Life on a
WAGON TRAIN

By Kristen Rajczak

Gareth Stevens
Publishing

Please visit our website, www.garethstevens.com. For a free color catalog of all our high-quality books, call toll free 1-800-542-2595 or fax 1-877-542-2596.

Library of Congress Cataloging-in-Publication Data

Rajczak, Kristen.
 Life on a wagon train / Kristen Rajczak.
      p. cm. — (What you didn't know about history)
 Includes index.
 ISBN 978-1-4339-8445-7 (pbk.)
 ISBN 978-1-4339-8446-4 (6-pack)
 ISBN 978-1-4339-8444-0 (library binding)
 1. Frontier and pioneer life—West (U.S.)—Juvenile literature. 2. Overland journeys to the Pacific—Juvenile literature. 3. Pioneers—West (U.S.)—History—19th century—Juvenile literature. 4. West (U.S.)—History—19th century—Juvenile literature. 5. West (U.S.)—Social life and customs—19th century—Juvenile literature. I. Title.
 F596.R33 2013
 978'.02—dc23
                                            2012031288

First Edition

Published in 2013 by
Gareth Stevens Publishing
111 East 14th Street, Suite 349
New York, NY 10003

Copyright © 2013 Gareth Stevens Publishing

Designer: Dan Hosek and Michael J. Flynn
Editor: Kristen Rajczak

Photo credits: Cover, pp. 1, 21 MPI/Archive Photos/Getty Images; p. 5 Photo Researchers/ Getty Images; pp. 7, 11 SuperStock/Getty Images; p. 9 Kean Collection/Archive Photos/ Getty Images; pp. 13, 17 James L. Amos/National Geographic/Getty Images; p. 15 Transcendental Graphics/Archive Photos/Getty Images; p. 19 N. Currier/ The Bridgeman Art Library/Getty Images.

Printed in the United States of America

CPSIA compliance information: Batch #CW13GS: For further information contact Gareth Stevens, New York, New York at 1-800-542-2595.

CONTENTS

Circle the Wagons 4

Getting Started 6

Chips for the Fire 8

Walkin' and Oxen 10

Tough Times 12

Staying Alive 14

Keeping in Touch 16

Trail Eats 18

Joy Along the Way 20

Glossary 22

For More Information 23

Index 24

Words in the glossary appear in **bold** type the first time they are used in the text.

CIRCLE THE WAGONS

From the 1840s to the 1880s, hundreds of thousands of Americans set out for the **frontier** outfitted with only what they could carry or fit in a covered wagon. For many, leaving family, friends, and homes behind was as hard as the overland journey they would take west. Others saw crossing the country as a great adventure!

Have you heard of the Oregon Trail? The 2,000-mile (3,218 km) **route** was one of the most popular ways for wagon trains to take.

Did You Know?

People leaving their homes to live in another place, such as those in wagon trains, are called emigrants.

The routes used by many wagon trains started as trails made by Native Americans.

GETTING STARTED

Wagon trains were often made up of families and people from the same town. They might have had more than 100 wagons or as few as two or three. Some emigrants painted their wagons bright colors to make it easier to keep a group together on the trails!

Men who had **explored** the frontier before, such as fur trappers, served as guides for some wagon trains. They gathered their wagon trains at several "jumping-off points," including places in Iowa and Missouri, before officially starting west.

Did You Know?

People starting out with a wagon train sometimes chose a leader and made a list of rules everyone had to follow.

Traveling in a group was safer as there were more people to help with sickness, wagon repairs, and possible Native American attacks.

CHIPS FOR THE FIRE

A wagon train's journey commonly took about 5 months. Each wagon had to be packed with food and supplies needed for the trip in addition to anything they needed to settle in the West. This meant leaving a lot behind—but wagons still weighed about 2,500 pounds (1,135 kg) each!

Families brought candles, tents, and tools to repair their wagon. They also brought pans to cook in. Luckily, they didn't need to bring wood for cooking fires. Buffalo chips—or dried buffalo waste—burned quickly and easily!

Did You Know?

Emigrants brought herds of sheep and cattle on the wagon train with them. They could become a source of food if needed and helped start livestock herds on the frontier.

Those traveling by wagon train ate dinner early so they could go to bed! It was important to be well rested for the hard journey.

WALKIN' AND OXEN

One of the most important decisions an emigrant family had to make was whether to buy mules, horses, or oxen to pull their wagon. Many chose oxen because they could pull heavier loads and generally cost less to care for. They were also less likely to be stolen by Native Americans.

However, the oxen pulled wagons full of supplies—not people. Unless someone was very old or very sick, travelers had to walk next to the wagon. One emigrant wrote that she went through 10 pairs of shoes during her journey to the West!

Did You Know?

When the weather was good and the land not too rough, most wagon trains could travel 12 to 20 miles (19 to 32 km) in a day.

An ox is a kind of male cow.

11

TOUGH TIMES

From dealing with unpleasant weather to crossing dangerously fast rivers, everyday life on a wagon train was full of struggles. Families knew it was a risky journey, but most felt free farmland, possible gold, or just starting over in a new place was worth it.

But on the way west, children and other slow travelers often got lost. Drowning and other **accidents** were common, too. Women's skirts got caught under wheels, pulling them under the wagon. People mistakenly fired guns at themselves and others.

Did You Know?

About one in 10 emigrants who traveled the Oregon Trail died along the way.

Wagon trains sometimes built rafts to float across a river. Other times, they drove right through the water!

STAYING ALIVE

One of the most common causes of death on wagon trains was **disease**. The lack of fresh fruits and vegetables gave many people an illness called scurvy. They also faced smallpox, a sickness somewhat like chicken pox.

From 1849 to 1852, thousands of emigrants died from cholera, a disease caused by **bacteria**. Historians think cholera spread because of the dirty conditions where people would stop for water. Today, we know boiling water kills the bacteria and could have stopped the spread of cholera.

Each family on the wagon train needed to bring more than 1,000 pounds (454 kg) of food.

19

JOY ALONG THE WAY

Though life on the wagon train was often tiring and hard, travelers still found ways to have a good time. They sang and told stories around the campfire. They **celebrated** weddings at jumping off points and along the trail. Most wagon trains had many new babies born on the way west, too!

Those traveling on the wagon train saw many parts of the growing United States. While the way wasn't always easy, it was always near some beautiful sights.

Did You Know?
Some children did schoolwork when the wagon train stopped for the day. Others took a few months off from school altogether!

Fun Facts About Life on a Wagon Train

- Many wagon trains didn't travel on Sunday mornings. Some didn't travel on Sundays at all!

- Men often brought guns along to hunt, but also to guard against Native American attacks. There were lots of gun accidents because many didn't know how to use the guns well.

- While free and easy to find, buffalo chips weren't the best fuel for a fire. Two to three **bushels** were needed to heat one meal!

- Dried meat, fruit, and bread were commonly eaten along the trail. They had to be soaked in water in order to be soft enough to eat.

LOSSARY

accident: an unexpected event that happens by chance

bacteria: tiny creatures that can only be seen with a microscope

bushel: a unit of measurement. One bushel equals about 9 gallons (35 l).

celebrate: to honor with special activities

churn: to stir or shake forcefully

disease: illness

explore: to search in order to find out new things

frontier: the edge of a settled part of a country

heirloom: something handed down through a family over many years

route: a course that people travel

*F*OR MORE INFORMATION

Books

Lusted, Marcia Amidon. *The Oregon Trail*. Edina, MN: ABDO Publishing, 2012.

Sechrist, Darren. *Westward, Ho!* New York, NY: Crabtree Publishing Company, 2009.

Todras, Ellen H. *Wagon Trains and Settlers*. New York, NY: Kingfisher, 2011.

Websites

The Oregon Trail
www.america101.us/trail/Oregontrail.html
Use this website to learn more about the Oregon Trail with videos, links, diaries of travelers, and more.

Trails & Territories
www.pbs.org/weta/thewest/places/trails_ter/index.htm
Read about many different trails and parts of the United States that wagon trains would have encountered.

INDEX

accidents 12, 21
babies 20
buffalo chips 8, 9, 21
butter 18
cattle 8, 18
cholera 14
death 12, 14
diaries 16
drowning 12
emigrants 4, 6, 8, 10, 12,
    14, 16, 18
food 8, 18, 19, 21
frontier 4, 6
fur trappers 6
guides 6
guns 12, 21
laundry 18
leader 6
letters 17

medicines 15
messages 16
milk 18
Native Americans 5, 7, 10,
    21
Oregon Trail 4, 12
oxen 10, 11
rules 6
schoolwork 20
scurvy 14
sheep 8
sickness 7, 10, 14, 15
smallpox 14
Sunday 18, 21
supplies 8, 10
weddings 20